CITIZENSHIP IN THE COMMUNITY

By Keith Monroe
Historian of the Boy Scouts of America

1977 Printing of the
1972 Edition

BOY SCOUTS OF AMERICA
NORTH BRUNSWICK, NEW JERSEY

Requirements

1. Tell how you would describe your town to a Scout from another state. Give a short history of your town. Tell about its ethnic and other groups, the economy, and the culture. Describe the future of your town.

2. Mark or point out on a map of your town the following:

   (a) Chief government buildings.
   (b) Fire station, police station, and hospital nearest your home.
   (c) Schools, churches, and synagogues near your home.
   (d) Main highways to neighboring cities and towns.
   (e) Nearest railroads and bus stations and airport, if any.
   (f) Chief industries or other major places of employment.
   (g) Historical and other interesting points.

3. Make a list of community problems. Pick one in your community. From newspapers, news broadcasts, or other kinds of public information and talk, gather ideas on both sides of your chosen problem. Give your own ideas on it.

4. Chart the organization of your state government. Show all three branches. Tell what each does.

5. Do one of the following:

   (a) Chart the organization of your village, town, city, or county government. Show top officers, courts, and departments. Show which officers are elected and which are appointed.
   (b) Tell how to do seven of the following in your community:
   (1) Report a fire.
   (2) Report an automobile accident.
   (3) Call an ambulance.
   (4) Report damage to electric power, gas, or water system.
   (5) Report damage to or need of repair on streets, roads, bridges, or sewage system.
   (6) Get a bicycle license.

Copyright © 1972
Boy Scouts of America
North Brunswick, New Jersey
Library of Congress
Catalog Card Number: 19-600
ISBN 0-8395-3253-9
No. 3253
Printed in U.S.A.   30M277

(7) Get a dog license.
(8) Report a contagious disease.
(9) Report a mad dog scare.
(10) Get a building permit.
(11) Call a veterinarian.
(12) Get help from your county agricultural agent.
(c) Visit one department of your local government. Report on what services it does for the community. Or, attend a court session or a public meeting of a government body. Report on what took place.

6. Tell how much it costs to run your local government for 1 year. Tell where the money comes from. Outline for what it is chiefly spent. What kind of taxes do your family and others in your community pay to meet this cost?

7. Show that you have taken an active part in elections of your officers and matters of business in groups to which you belong.

8. List and describe the work of five volunteer organizations through which people of your community work together for the general good. Do something for or take part in the activities of one of these organizations other than Scouting.

9. Do one of the following:

(a) Name the main political parties in your community or state. Explain their different points of view on one public issue.
(b) Describe one job in your community in some form of public service. Tell what qualifications you need for the job.

10. Do one of the following:

(a) Draw the course of your home water supply from watershed to water tap and on to receiving stream. Show waste treatment, if any.
(b) Find out if the water supply is likely to be a problem in your town in the future. Explain why.
(c) Take part in a community or troop recycling project.
(d) Give a talk to your troop or school class on what the individual can do to conserve energy.

3

11. Define water pollution. Give the main causes and results of water pollution nationally and in your town. Find out what steps, if any, are taken to control pollution in your area. Tell what other steps might be taken.

12. Tell how good land-use planning can conserve energy and why it is important to five of the following: community planners, highway builders, camp planners, small landowners, farmers, ranchers, recreation planners, industrial and housing developers, fishermen, and hunters.

13. Do the following:

   (a) List and explain at least five privileges and forms of protection you enjoy as a citizen in your community. Describe your obligations to the community.
   (b) Plan your own program of community service. Get approval of your plan from your Scoutmaster and counselor. Give 5 hours of your time in carrying it out. Or, give 5 hours of community service as part of a troop project.

Contents

A Tenderfoot, a Citizen? 5
Your Community's Past, Present, and Future   8
Learning Your Way Around   16
Your Community's Problems   18
Your State Government   22
Your Local Government   24
Paying for Government   28
Doing Your Part   32
Volunteers for Service   34
Politics and Public Service   38
Your Community's Water Supply   41
Planning for Land Use   44
Your Community and You   47
Books About Citizenship in the Community   48

A Tenderfoot, a Citizen?

Why should an 11-year-old Tenderfoot Scout like me tell how I passed the merit badge in Citizenship in the Community? Good question. I'm not Superkid.

I guess the answer could be that I got extra-good advice while I was working for the badge. This advice might help you.

Some guys in my troop have another answer. Or maybe it's the same answer plus a little poison ivy. They say that when something is explained so I can understand, then anybody can understand it.

We'll see. Anyhow, I know for sure that nobody can get this badge just by memorizing what I say. Getting Citizenship in the Community takes legwork on your own. It takes some asking around in your neighborhood and maybe farther. That's because every town is different, every city is different. But in any community there are people who are glad to help you understand — if you just ask. That's how it was with me. And I know Scouts who found people like that in other places.

The man who helped me most is Judge James E. Wise. I got to know him because of my afternoon paper route.

I like to get acquainted with people. I guess Judge Wise does too. So when I stopped by to collect payment, we had a chat. That was when I found out he is a retired judge. I also found out that he is even more interested in Scouting than I am.

"Did you know that I'm a merit badge counselor for the citizenship merit badges?" he said. "Now that a Scout must earn one merit badge as part of the Tenderfoot requirements, I'll be looking for you to get Citizenship in the Community."

I laughed. "Thanks for the compliment, Judge Wise. Maybe I look old enough to vote and pay taxes, but I'm not. I'll have to wait quite a few years before I start thinking about being a citizen."

He stared at me, "Mike, do you actually mean to say that you don't know you're a citizen? Didn't anyone ever explain that you've been a citizen of the United States ever since the day you were born here?"

"Aw, well, maybe I'm called a citizen. But kids my age don't count in running the city, or in anything that

5

real full-grown citizens do."

"You say kids don't count? Then why do you think the city builds schools and playgrounds for you? Why is there a special section of the public library for kids? Why do people start Scout troops for you? Let me tell you, Mike, kids count for a lot in every community."

If somebody wants to argue, I'll argue with him, even if he is a judge. So I shot back, "Oh, sure, people do a lot for us. That's because they want us to grow up to be good citizens, right? But at my age we don't do anything that real citizens do."

"Hmm. You said a minute ago that you're not old enough to pay taxes. But when you bought your bicycle, a sales tax was part of what you paid. Whenever you buy a hamburger or go to a movie, you pay taxes."

"Well, okay, so I'm a taxpayer, sort of. But isn't that the closest I come to being a real citizen?"

Maybe I was too fresh, talking back to Judge Wise that way. But he didn't seem to mind. I could see he enjoyed our argument.

He said, "A citizen must reach a certain age before he can do certain things, like driving a car or running for mayor. But even at your age, a citizen has most of the rights that older citizens have."

I almost said, "Name a few," but I didn't. I wasn't *that* fresh. I just waited, hoping he would go on.

He did. "Think about it, Mike. Everyone born in America has these big important rights, like the right to be protected from lawbreakers. For example, if another kid were to steal something from you, there are laws to help you get it back. If a storekeeper cheated you, the law could step in. If you got hit by a car, the law might make the driver pay your hospital bills. In fact, if anyone harms you in any way, there are laws to help you."

He let all this sink in. Then he went on. "You have other rights as a citizen too. One of the biggest is your right to an education — in most other countries there isn't much free education, but there's plenty in America. You also have a right to use the roads and sidewalks; to use the public parks and public buildings; to get information from government offices."

I was ready to admit that I was a citizen sure enough, and that citizenship could be important to kids. But the judge was just getting warmed up. He went on:

"Here's another example. Suppose something terrible happened that made you an orphan. Then the government would take steps to see that someone took care of you. It would also make sure that you got your rightful share of whatever your parents had owned.

"Or let's imagine another really bad case," he continued. "Suppose your parents were sick and out of work and broke. The government has public hospitals for citizens who find themselves in that kind of trouble. And it has unemployment insurance that will pay them a little money. And it also has offices that will try hard to help them find work as soon as they're able to work. In the meantime it could be helping you too. In fact, our lawmakers have done their best to make sure that any citizen who really needs food or medical care or a place to live can be helped to get them. This is all part of what it means to be an American citizen. So don't ever think you're not a real citizen."

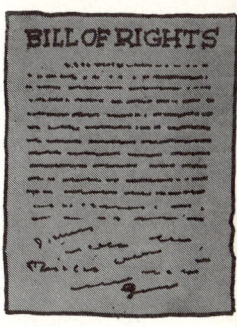

He went on about the Bill of Rights, which he said gave me freedom of speech and freedom of religion, and other freedoms. But this was over my head, so I won't try to tell you what he said. If you're old enough to understand those rights of citizens, great. You'll probably want to know about them. But don't ask me. Go ask somebody who knows. Or look in a library.

Finally Judge Wise sat back. "Well, young man, you needled me into giving a lecture. I hope I didn't waste my breath."

I grinned. "You opened up my head. I'm glad you're taking time to tell me what citizenship is all about."

"I only showed you part of the picture," he said. I told you what you can *get* as a citizen, but not what you should *give*. In other words, we talked about your rights, but not about your responsibilities."

"No problem," I said. "I'll be telling about the rights and responsibilities of a citizen when I pass another Tenderfoot requirement, the Citizenship skill award."

"I know," he said. "So why don't you finish up that skill award and then keep going to get Citizenship in the Community for Tenderfoot? It's required for First Class anyhow, so why not get it now?"

Well, sure. He gave me such a push that I figured I'd like to go on. So I looked up the requirements.

Man, what a jolt! I almost gave up when I read the very first requirement for Citizenship in the Community.

Your Community's Past, Present, and Future

1. Tell how you would describe your town to a Scout from another state. Give a short history of your town. Tell about its ethnic and other groups, the economy, and the culture. Describe the future of your town.

Ethnic? What's ethnic? I never heard of it.
Economy? Did that mean saving your money? or what? and why?
Culture? No culture in our town, for all I could see.
Future? Was I a fortuneteller?
The next time I saw Judge Wise on his porch, I rode up to the steps and stopped a minute. Staring at the ground, I said, "Thanks for telling me about citizenship, Judge Wise. But I looked up the requirements for that merit badge — and there's no way I could pass. Just the first requirement is too much. I'd have to learn the history of the city. I'm no good at history. Too many dates to memorize."

He chuckled. "Go back and read the requirement again, Mike. It doesn't mention dates. It doesn't say you have to memorize. If I planned to tell someone about the history of a place, I would look it up and make some notes. I'd keep the notes handy while I talked. I wouldn't depend on memory."

So then I brought up those puzzlers like "ethnic."
He said, "It's not as hard as it sounds, Mike. Tell you what. Some afternoon when you finish your newspaper route, come back here and we'll talk over the requirement. I know you can pass it if you try."

Well, he was so friendly, and so enthused about citizenship, how could I disappoint him? So a few days later I went back. We sat on his porch and I showed him the brain-buster first requirement for the merit badge.

"Let's take it one part at a time," he said. "Do you know any boy in some other state?"

"Sure. My cousin Phil lives in Chicago, Ill."

"Let's say you want Phil to come and spend a vacation here. What would you tell him about our city?"

"Oh, I guess I'd tell about our places to swim and skate, and the hikes we could take —"

The judge stopped me. "You're on the right track. No need to tell me all you'd say. If you sat down with pencil and paper for 10 minutes, you could make quite a long list of things that Phil would like to know. He'd wonder what sort of weather to expect. He'd wonder what the kids are like — are they mostly black or white, Jewish, Indian, rich or poor, or what? Maybe he'd want to know whether it's crowded here, because he comes from a crowded city. Maybe he'd wonder whether most families live in houses with yards or blocks of small houses all the same or in big buildings, or whatever. He'd be interested in whether we ride subways to get places or do we ride buses or would he need a bike here?"

I nodded. "Okay, that part isn't so tough. But what about the history? Ugh."

Frowning, Judge Wise said, "Too many boys think history is a list of dates to memorize. I've already told you not to depend on memory for this. Jot down the important facts when you find them. You can have them with you when you're passing the merit badge. And if I were you, I wouldn't pay too much attention to dates. History is mainly people, not dates."

I nodded and sighed. "Shakespeare and George Washington and all that."

His frown deepened. "I don't mean a list of names. Use your head, Mike. Ask yourself questions about people—then you'll get interested in them. For example, what kind of people started our town? Were they jailbirds or pirates, like the men who started a few towns? Were they restless types who never settled down? Were they big ranchers? Or were they ambitious pioneers who wanted to own their own small farms? Or were they something else? Why did they pick this spot? Were they looking for gold or furs or the Fountain of Youth or more plentiful hunting or what? How did they get along with the Indians, and with newcomers?"

"Hey, it might be fun to find out," I said. "Where can I look?"

"Go to the library and ask. But first do some detective work on your own. Prowl around town, use your eyes, and write up a list of names to ask about."

My brain was revving up. "You mean, who are the streets named after? And the park downtown—the man it was named for?"

"Sure. Why are the statues to certain people around town? Look at buildings and check on their names. If there's a Bennett Hall, then someone named Bennett must have done big things. Every town is full of old names. And the names stand for interesting people—mostly people who made a real difference here."

"Can do," I said. "But what about ethnic and those others? They really rock me back."

He gave his low chuckle again. "Well, yes, I guess the word ethnic might be new to you. The requirement says to tell about your town's ethnic and other groups. The key word is 'groups.' You need to know what an ethnic group is. There's a saying, 'Birds of a feather flock together.' Ever hear it?"

I nodded.

"What does it mean?" he demanded.

"I guess it means that guys who are pretty much the same will run around together."

"Exactly. Good way to explain it, Mike. Now then—can you think of any group of people in this city who are pretty much the same, and who stick together quite a bit?"

I thought it over. "How about the people who put on that folk dance festival last month? Don't they come from Sweden?"

"At least they come from Sweden or other Scandinavian countries near Sweden. They're a good example of an ethnic group, because they do lots of things together, and because they're alike in various ways. Can you tell me a few ways we can recognize Scandinavians as birds of a feather?"

That question stumped me. I shook my head.

"Think a minute, Mike," he pressed. "Some of those families are on your paper route, I know. The children are probably in your school. Are the children alike in any ways?"

"Well, a lot of them seem to have yellow hair and blue eyes. And oh yes, their names mostly end in -son, like Peterson and Johannson and Erlandson."

"Good! Keep on thinking. Do you ever see groups of these families together?"

Finally it hit me. "Why, sure! Plenty of them go to the Lutheran church. And there's a restaurant called Little Scandia, where I see them."

"All right. So now you've told me about one ethnic group. Think of another ethnic group around here."

"How about Orientals? They have their own churches and meeting places. And lots of them live near McKinley School, I think."

"Good. Now you've started, you can probably think of three or four other groups that stick together fairly closely."

I thought of Little Italy. And Negroes. And all the Jews who cluster near Sinai Temple and the Beth Sholom synagogue. And the families from Mexico who live in the southwest part of town.

When I slowed down, Judge Wise said, "What was so hard in telling about ethnic groups? You thought of six without half trying. Probably you could find six more if you put your mind to it."

I mumbled, "I just didn't know what ethnic meant." I felt dumb for not having tried to find out.

"Ethnic means of the same race, or sometimes speaking the same language and coming from the same part of the world. If you moved to Mexico, you'd probably spend a lot of time with any other people from the United States who lived near you—so you'd be in your own ethnic group. But we're not quite finished with this requirement. You have to tell about some other groups besides ethnic groups."

He waited for me to go on. I couldn't. I hadn't any clue to what he wanted.

Finally he said, "There are lots of reasons besides nationality or race that bring folks together in groups. In a college town, the students are a separate group from the townspeople. In a summer resort, the year-round people are different from the summer people. Then, too, sometimes people have religious ties that pull them together. The Mormons felt like that when they moved into Utah. Or take the Amish or the House of David or the Dunkers."

He waited again. I saw he wanted me to think of other groups. I thought awhile. "How about people that do the same kind of work? Could you call them a group?"

"You might, if they seem to stick together in other ways besides their jobs. What people were you thinking

about?"

"The people who work at the cannery. Most of them seem to live near each other. I see them at the same bowling alleys and in the same park over on the North Side. I know they're from the cannery because they wear their union button. Or sometimes they wear those jackets from the cannery's baseball and volleyball teams."

"Good eye, Mike. You notice and remember things as you move around town. That's a very, very important part of citizenship. You'll notice other groups when you look more closely. Well, let's get along. The next part of the requirement is to tell about the economy of our city. Can you do that?"

"You mean how the city saves money?"

"No. Economy means more than that. In this sentence it covers whatever is important to people when they think about profit and loss. So, in telling about our community, you should be able to tell whether any neighborhoods are expensive to live in, and whether some other neighborhoods have very low costs. What about rents? What about real estate prices? What about grocery prices? Are taxes higher here, or lower, than in other towns? Are jobs hard to find? Or is work plentiful? What kinds of work? Do most people have automobiles? Do many homes have swimming pools or tennis courts? Are there many vacant houses, empty buildings, unrented offices? Are the taxpayers getting good service from the departments that use tax money, like the fire department, garbage collection, street repairs, and so on?"

He was popping questions like a machine gun. Once again I felt ready to quit. "Probably I'm dumb, but I just can't answer any of those questions, Judge."

"Of course not," he said sharply. "At your age, boys don't know about jobs and rents and all that. But you can easily find out. Ask your mother and dad whether this is a good place to live, from the money angle, or whether they would like to move away. Ask them about taxes and the other questions I mentioned."

I pulled out my pocket notebook and began scribbling down the questions so I wouldn't forget.

"Other people can help you too," he added. "The chamber of commerce, for example. Someone there will give you a lot of answers, if you just explain why you want to know. Furthermore, almost any elected city official here will know plenty about the economy of our city. Telephone his office. You may not get to talk to him, but I'll bet he has assistants and secretaries who answer questions from the public every day. Or ask some real estate men."

I looked at the merit badge requirement again. "The next thing is culture," I said. "My teacher at school says this isn't a really cultured city compared to places like Boston or like Carmel in California."

"Maybe so. Your teacher meant the kind of culture that supports symphony orchestras or art shows or garden parties at beautiful old homes. But the word culture is used differently in this merit badge requirement. Here it means describing how people live in the community, and especially how they spend their free time."

I scratched my head. How should I know what people did when they were off work? Was I a detective?

He went on, "Remember, Mike, in this whole Requirement 1 you should imagine that you're telling someone like your cousin Phil whatever he'd like to know about this city. He wants to know how different the living is here.

I shrugged. "It's entirely different in every way. Right?"

"Oh, you're mostly right. But you probably see the same movies and TV shows."

"Not really. He can get more TV channels. And he's close to more movie theaters."

The judge's white head nodded briskly. "Good point. I hadn't thought of that. It's one more difference between the Chicago culture and ours. You know, this matter of local cultures is really surprising when you get into it. Did you ever stop to think how many differences there must be between a city that has an airport and a city that doesn't? Or between a town that has few visitors and a town where crowds of tourists stop?"

"There must be a jillion different kinds of town," I said. "I've read about mining towns, and farm towns, and river towns like the one where Tom Sawyer lived."

"Of course. And a Southern town would have many differences from a New England town, wouldn't it? Maybe you know families who moved here from other parts of the country. Can you see any differences in the way they act or the way they seem to think?"

"Well, I know a kid who lived in a beach town in California. He says everything was different there—the schools, the sports they played, the public parks, they way people dressed, how they traveled, even the foods they ate. And I guess his family has different ideas about politics and religion than most families here."

"All right then. You know how to pass the requirement about our culture. You've seen other places on television and in movies. You've read about other places. And you've visited still other places. Just ask yourself, what's different about this city. Then tell Phil why you'd rather live here—or why you don't like living here, if you want to gripe."

The sun had set, and my brain felt as if it had been through an eggbeater. So I stood up and thanked Judge Wise, we shook hands, and I went home.

That was how I got into the merit badge for Citizenship in the Community. I still wasn't sure I could pass. But if the judge would help me understand what I needed to do, why not give it a try?

There's a Scout in my patrol that I hang around with. He's older than I am, but we get along fine. We see each other all the time, because we live nearby. I asked him, "Want to work on Citizenship in the Community? We could help each other."

His name is Steve. "Man, you picked one that takes weeks to pass," Steve said. "But my pop says citizenship is everybody's business, even mine. He says it takes a long time to make yourself a good citizen. So I guess we oughtta get with it. How do we start?"

I showed him the first requirement, and he read the line about town history. He asked if I'd tried the library. I had. "There were more books about early settlers than you could carry home," I told him. "Not strictly about our city, but about our part of the state."

"All right, that's a start. Let me copy the notes you got from the books. It doesn't matter whether I get facts from the books or from you, does it? Then I'll go around and talk to some old-timers in town and tell you what I find out. By dividing up the legwork, we'll learn more."

I asked Judge Wise and he said if we really understood each other's notes, we could share them. Steve got some good history from old people his grandmother knows. It was interesting to hear why most of them stayed here when hard times hit the town.

As my share of the detective work I tried the newspaper. I hit a jackpot there. The paper had printed a special edition on the day the city was a hundred years old, and I found so much surprising stuff that I could have made up a whole TV special about the history of this place.

"We forgot one thing," Steve said, just when I thought we had Requirement 1 all wrapped up. "The requirement says we've got to describe the town's future."

I giggled. "Let's predict that they'll move the capital from Washington, D.C., right here to our good old hometown. And then let's say an earthquake will wipe it out."

Steve smiled, but he said, "Come on, you can't be that stupid. Your friend Judge Wise would ask you why you think so. We need reasons for whatever we predict. What do we really think this city will be like when we're old?"

"Aw, who knows, Steve? Everybody might move away and leave it a ruin. Or it might keep building up and get swallowed in a bigger city."

"Well, which is the trend? Shrinking or growing? and why?"

I remembered a tip from Judge Wise. "Let's ask the chamber of commerce or some realtors. They know what's been happening here—and maybe they see some changes ahead."

That was a good tip. We saw the plans for a lake they're going to make, not far from here. And we heard about some companies that plan to move here. So now I know why more people will probably move here, and more people may stay nearby on vacations. I may even start a business here myself when I'm old enough, because I should get plenty of customers.

Learning Your Way Around

2. Mark or point out on a map of your town the following:

 (a) Chief government buildings.
 (b) Fire station, police station, and hospital nearest your home.
 (c) Schools, churches, and synagogues near your home.
 (d) Main highways to neighboring cities and towns.
 (e) Nearest railroads and bus stations and airport, if any.
 (f) Chief industries or other major places of employment.
 (g) Historical and other interesting points.

Marking the map was easy, once I found where we could get maps. After we tried service stations with no luck, we telephoned city hall and found that the chamber of commerce had free maps. But when I showed my marked-up map to Judge Wise, he wasn't satisfied.

"Hmm. Very neat," he murmured. "Where is the nearest Catholic church?"

"Right there," I said, pointing it out on the map.

"So I see. But what if you don't have the map handy? Put the map away. Now tell me how to find the nearest police station."

My jaw dropped. "The requirement only says to point it out on the map."

He shot me a frosty look. "In that case shall I just approve it, whether you've learned anything or not? All you want is the badge to wear?"

I saw he was disappointed in me, but I didn't know why. I just scuffed at the porch step and wondered what to say.

"Tell me something, Mike. You are working on this badge because you plan to be a good useful citizen. How do you think marking this map can help in citizenship?"

I mumbled, "Maybe I'm supposed to know where those buildings are?"

"When?"

"Whenever I need to know, I guess."

"Ah ha! Yes indeed! If strangers asked you how to find a hospital in a hurry, would you run home and look for your map?"

I got the point. So Steve and I studied our maps and tested each other until we could give directions without looking. But some of the practice still seemed useless to me. I grumbled to Steve, "Why do we need to know all this? Someone may want to get to a Baptist church in a big rush, or to the county hall of records?"

"Could be. Every place on this list could be important to somebody. If a man couldn't find the church, he might be late for a wedding. Or let's say he needed a bus station. If we gave him a bum steer, the bus might leave without him. And suppose he heard a job was open at the hall of records or the cannery or some other place on the list. If we sent him in the wrong direction, he might be too late to get the job."

Your Community's Problems

3. Make a list of community problems. Pick one in your community. From newspapers, news broadcasts, or other kinds of public information and talk, gather ideas on both sides of your chosen problem. Give your own ideas on it.

I asked Judge Wise, "What problems do we look for?"

"A community problem is something that needs improvement," he said. "This puts us into the heart of the merit badge. Improving the community is a big duty of every good citizen. Including you."

I figured the old judge was a little out of touch. So I tried to set him straight, in a nice way. "When it comes to improving the community, nobody listens to 11-year-olds," I explained. "Maybe they did when you were a boy, but that's all changed."

"When I was a boy, children were expected to be seen and not heard," he snapped. "We got a whole lot less attention than you do, Mike—even though most of us did a lot more work to help our parents. . . . Well, no matter. Our boyhood ideas about improving our town were half baked. We listened to any loud talker, and took our ideas from him. Don't you do the same?"

"Not really, Judge. Nowadays we kids hear a lot more, so we have sharper ideas. Take the schools. My ideas about them are the same as the man who talked about schools on television Sunday. And he's the state governor, so my ideas must be pretty good."

The judge laughed so hard he almost tipped over his rocking chair. "That's just what I mean! You swallowed the governor's line of talk. The ideas weren't yours at all."

"You mean you don't agree with what he said?"

"I don't know yet whether I agree with him or not. The real question is, why does he think as he does? Did he take all the important facts into account? Or did he overlook some facts? I'll bet you don't know. I'm sure I don't."

I tried to think up a comeback. Suddenly it looked as

if the judge had talked himself into a trap.

"A minute ago," I said slowly, "you said my duty as a citizen is to improve the community. But then didn't you sort of reverse yourself? Didn't you say my ideas for improving it were half baked? How can I improve the city with half-baked ideas that I swallow from television?"

He rubbed his chin. "You may make a good lawyer someday, young man. At least you pay attention to the argument. My point was that youngsters tend to believe any speaker who sounds loud and simple and important. Many older people are likely to believe him, too. It's human nature to form opinions quickly, on very few facts—or just on a slogan, with no facts at all. Then our opinions may get set in concrete. We pay no attention to anything that could change our minds. We refuse to think we could be wrong."

I knew what he meant, all right. Some guys won't even listen to both sides of a record. I asked the judge, "How can you say that kids should improve the community, when nobody listens to us? We don't sound loud and important."

"Well, of course you can make this a better city by doing Good Turns like cleaning up litter or clearing away a fire hazard or phoning police when you see something they should know."

"But Judge, this requirement says to study community problems! It tells me to get ideas on both sides, then give my own ideas. Why? Who cares about my ideas?"

"It doesn't say you must give your ideas to city officials. As you pointed out, they probably wouldn't listen."

"Okay. So why should I bother?"

He said, "You should bother for the same reason you practice pitching if you want to be a pitcher someday."

"Uh, could you explain a little more, Judge Wise?"

"Getting your own ideas on civic questions is mostly training for the future, Mike. To give you practice in sizing up problems. To cure you of taking sides too fast. To help you form the habit of asking for more facts. Then you'll be better prepared when people are ready to listen to you."

"However," he added, "don't be so sure they'll *never* listen now. If you were to write a letter to a newspaper, telling some facts that people had overlooked about a local problem, your letter might get printed and get talked about."

"Well, my own problem is Requirement 3. How do I make up a list of local problems? If this community has problems, nobody told me."

His lips tightened. "Mike, sometimes you sound like a crybaby. Use your head. The words of the requirement itself tell where to find problems: 'from newspapers, news broadcasts, or other kinds of public information and talk.'"

"They're mostly about national problems and world problems," I said.

"Partly, but not all. You'll find what you need, if you look through the whole paper or pick the right broadcasts. Look at the editorials in the newspaper. Look at the 'letters to the editor' section. Don't you realize that nobody believes any city is perfect, that everyone wants some changes? Listen to the talk at school, to the talk at your own supper table. Or if you really want an earful, go and sit in the audience at some public meeting—the city council, maybe; or a board of education meeting; or the public-forum type of get-together, where rival candidates speak or where various important people discuss some local question."

"How do I find out about these meetings?" I asked.

"In the newspapers you'll see announcements of public meetings almost every day. Maybe the announcements sound dull, but at most meetings you'll hear lively arguments. They'll start you wondering. You'll also get interested in news reports of meetings you've attended — because often you'll find that the news focuses on statements which you didn't realize were important when you listened to them."

"**Okay, I see** how to get together a list of local problems," I said. "But after I make the list, how should I choose which problem to concentrate on?"

"Your own interest will guide you. Wait until you come across a subject that whets your curiosity. As you build up a list of things you think should be improved, something will probably click. You'll think to yourself, 'Now *there* is something I wish they'd fix—but I wonder which is the best way to fix it?' It might be too many accidents or near-accidents on a street near you. It might be smoke that keeps smudging your neighborhood. Or it might be something that worries many more people, like a plan to tear down several blocks of buildings and put something else there, or a question about the best route for a new expressway near you, or whether the city should borrow money to enlarge the airport."

"I'll go over the list with Steve," I said. "Maybe we'll find a question we disagree on. Then we can study up for a debate with each other."

"That sounds promising," the judge said. "But when you've picked your problem, and you begin to gather ideas about various ways of solving it, you'll find there are two kinds of ideas. Some are facts; some are opinions. Both are important. But get all the facts you can. You'll find that some opinions don't fit the facts."

When I told Steve what the judge said, we found a hole in the advice he gave me.

"What is a fact?" Steve challenged me.

"Well, it's what people know, instead of what they believe."

"Oh yeah? If somebody says, 'I know for a fact that the mayor is no good,' does that make it a fact?"

"Well, I guess you'd have to ask, 'How do you know?' " I said.

Steve said, "Then maybe he answers, 'Because I read it in the paper,' or 'The TV broadcast said so.' Now is it a fact?"

We looked it up in the dictionary. It said, "A truth known by actual observation or experience." But we can't observe most facts. If anyone else says he observes something, can we be sure?

I asked the judge. But he just said, "Even when you see something for yourself, there may be more than meets your eye. Maybe something else happened earlier or later that gives a different meaning to what you saw. Maybe someone is trying to do something very different than you think he is. So the best you can do is to keep getting other viewpoints, to see if anybody challenges what you think is a fact. When you check with various people whose opinions are different, and they agree that certain information is true, then you're probably safe."

When we picked out a community problem and dug into it, we still got confused trying to sort out facts from hearsay. It shows that a guy should get plenty of viewpoints before he decides.

Your State Government

4. Chart the organization of your state government. Show all three branches. Tell what each does.*

I groaned when I saw the fourth requirement. "I thought this was Citizenship in the Community, not the state," I told Steve.

As usual his brain was a little deeper than mine. He said, "There isn't any merit badge for citizenship in the state. Probably they figure the community and the state sort of blend into each other."

"Maybe," I growled. "But I noticed by the newspapers that our mayor and our governor don't seem to agree on much."

"And our state senator disagrees with our state assemblyman. All the more reason why we oughtta understand what they're trying to do. They all want a flock of votes from our city, don't they? And the city needs dough from the state taxes."

"Yeah. But I don't vote, and I don't decide where my tax money goes. So why should I think about state government?"

"Oh Mike, you're like a guy in a canoe, asking why think about the winds or currents! Most laws we follow here are state laws. Our city elects some of the people who make those laws. Our city helps elect a governor who can block a law with his veto."

Okay, okay! When I worry about laws, I'll worry about our state."

"You better worry sooner. Don't you know the state reaches into every neighborhood from a dozen angles? It can run a highway through here. It can close down a camping ground outside of town, or open new ones. It can send soldiers into town if there's a flood or riot or something. It can put a branch of the state university here. Man, there's excitement in state government. Get yourself a lineup and follow the game."

So I got a lineup—in other words, a chart of our state government. I did it alone, because Steve was sort of fed up with me and wouldn't help. In the school library I found a civics book with a chart like the one shown below, which gave me the general idea. Then I had to find out what the different departments and bureaus were in our own state, how many judges on the state supreme court, how many people in the legislature, and so on. When I asked the librarian, she handed me a manual of our state government, and from then on it was easy—but I can't say it was exciting. Oh well, maybe someday I'll be glad I know.

*The organization of state governments differ. Make sure you get the proper information for your state. Scouts who live in the District of Columbia or in a possession of the United States should chart the structure of that government.

Your Local Government

5. Do one of the following:

M (a) Chart the organization of your village, town, city, or county government. Show top officers, courts, and departments. Show which officers are elected and which are appointed.

M (b) Tell how to do seven of the following in your community:
  (1) Report a fire.
  (2) Report an automobile accident.
  (3) Call an ambulance.
  (4) Report damage to electric power, gas, or water system.
  (5) Report damage to or need of repair on streets, roads, bridges, or sewage system.
  (6) Get a bicycle license.
  (7) Get a dog license.
  (8) Report a contagious disease.
  (9) Report a mad dog scare.
  (10) Get a building permit.
  (11) Call a veterinarian.
  (12) Get help from your county agricultural agent.

(c) Visit one department of your local government. Report on what services it does for the community. Or, attend a court session or a public meeting of a government body. Report on what took place.

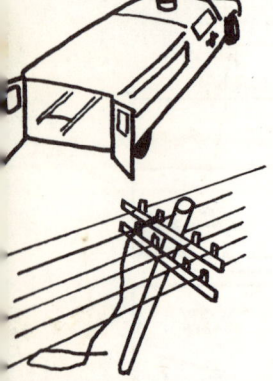

When I got to Requirement 5 I argued with myself. Which of the projects should I do?

I knew I could fix up a chart to pass 5a. I could find out at the information counter in city hall just how my town is organized.

Or 5b would be easy too, because I'd already earned the Family Living skill award for Tenderfoot, where I had to tell how to call for help in family emergencies. So I already knew that you can't get an ambulance just by phoning an ambulance company, and that most doctors won't leave the office and rush to your bedroom when you phone. In fact, I could pass seven of those 5b requirements with what I already knew.

But 5c looked harder, so I finally took it. Why did I pick the hard one? Well, Steve was still sore because he thought I ducked away from anything hard. And the judge had called me a crybaby. I'd show them.

Actually 5c wasn't hard either. In fact, it was the most fun in the whole merit badge. I sat in traffic court and got so interested I hated to leave. A few days later, when I was passing the judge's front porch, he called to me:

"Say, Mike! An investigating committee from the legislature has scheduled a hearing right here in town. It'll be a rough one. The chairman will have his hands full. I hope you'll go over there and see how a good chairman operates, because you may have to do it yourself someday."

So I went. Talk about excitement! I didn't understand much of what the committee was investigating, but I could see that people in the audience were trying to make trouble—heckling, cheering, booing, or even standing up and speechifying. It was against the rules, as the chairman said, but he let them "mouth off" for awhile, until most of the crowd was on his side. Then he ordered police to put a few troublemakers out of the room. There was less trouble after that.

So I really passed 5c twice, and I'm glad. It was better than a double feature at the movies.

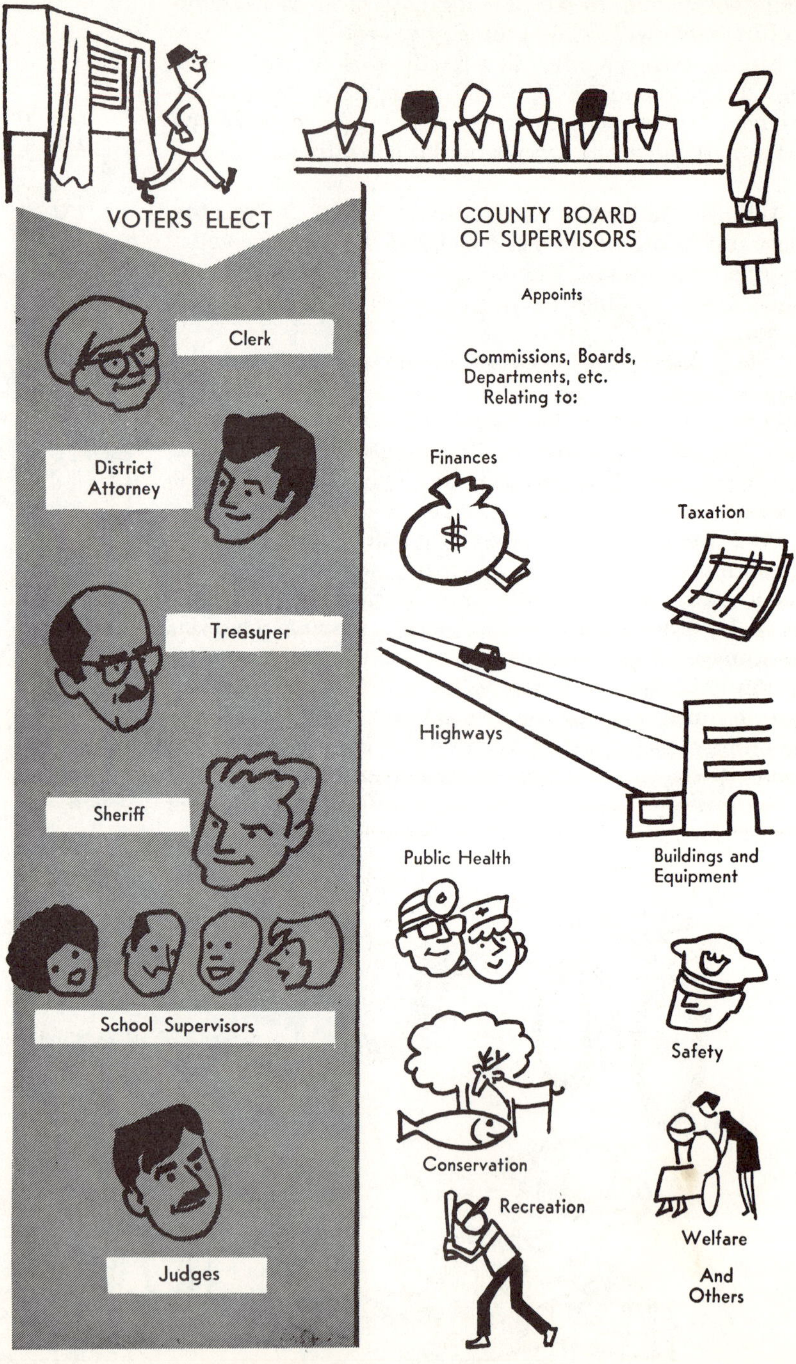

VOTERS ELECT

- Clerk
- District Attorney
- Treasurer
- Sheriff
- School Supervisors
- Judges

COUNTY BOARD OF SUPERVISORS

Appoints

Commissions, Boards, Departments, etc. Relating to:

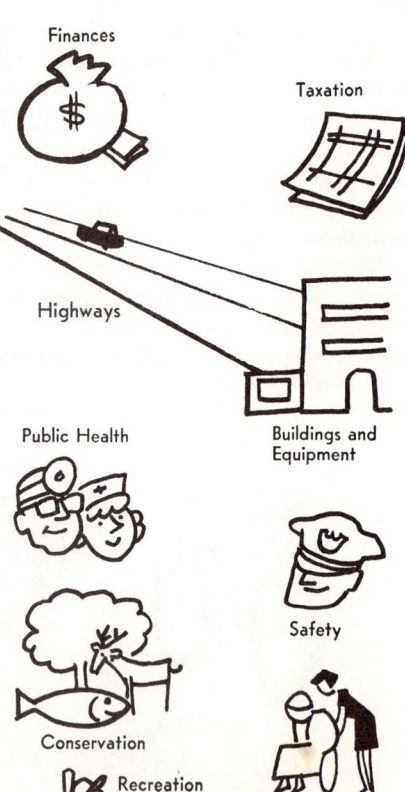

Finances

Taxation

Highways

Public Health

Buildings and Equipment

Safety

Conservation

Recreation

Welfare

And Others

VOTERS ELECT
BOARD OF EDUCATION
MAYOR
MUNICIPAL COURT JUDGES
Manager
COUNCIL
Departments
DPW
Health and Welfare
Public Works
Finance
Safety
Recreation
And Other Departments

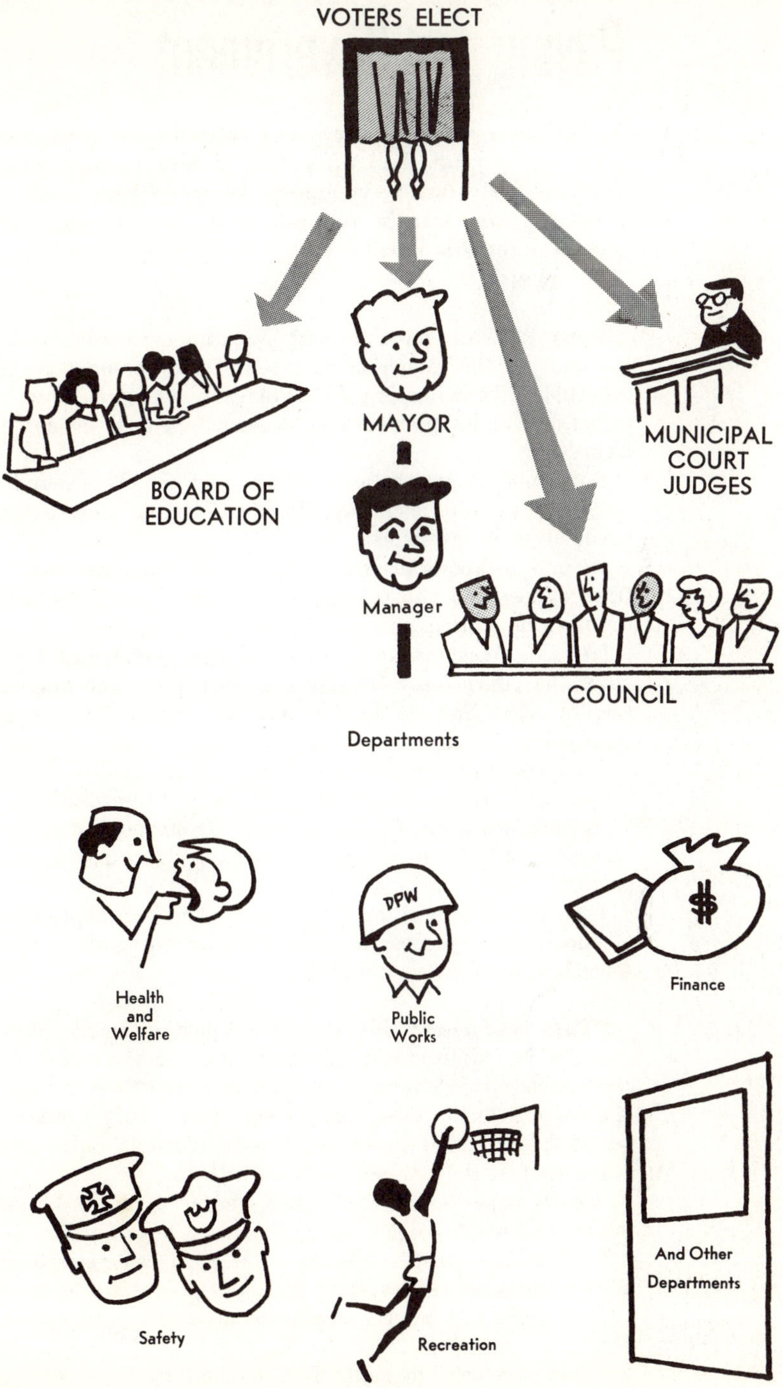

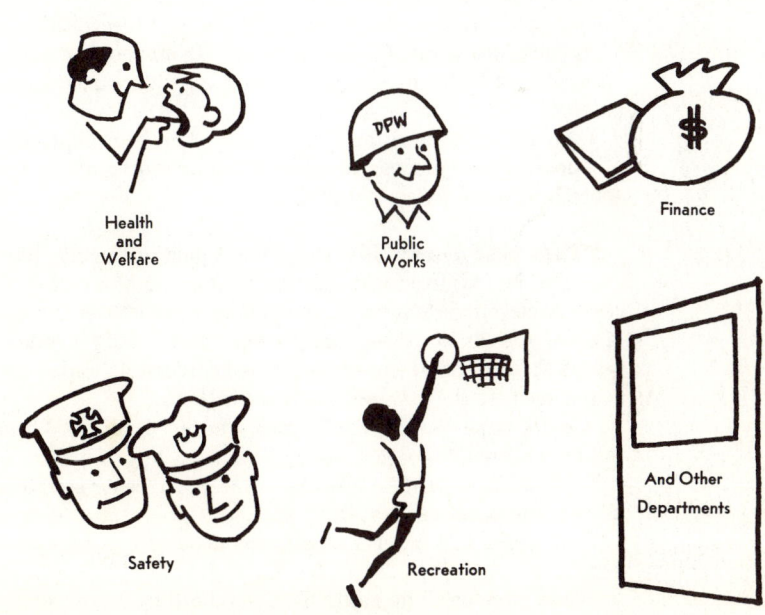

Paying for Government

6. Tell how much it costs to run your local government for 1 year. Tell where the money comes from. Outline for what it is chiefly spent. What kind of taxes do your family and others in your community pay to meet this cost?

Mayor

Judge Wise also gave me a tip on passing requirement 6. He told me the telephone number of the person who is responsible for collecting all the taxes in our town. When I called him and explained what I needed, he gave me some figures.

But I could hardly believe what he told me. "This sounds like we're a mighty rich city, Mr. Ross," I said. "How do we spend all these millions?"

He told me about keeping streets repaired and the cost of fire engines and the telephone bills for city offices and umpty-nine other expenses I'd never thought about.

He said, "We'd spend more, too, if some people had their way. The police think they should earn more, and maybe they're right. Some cities our size pay higher salaries to their police."

"How come we can't do the same?" I asked.

"We don't collect as much in taxes as those cities do. They pick up a heap of sales tax money from people passing through. And they have more industries, which are big taxpayers."

I thought of something. "Mr. Ross, when you mentioned all those city expenses, you didn't say anything about our schools. Don't they cost much?"

"They cost plenty. But they're not part of the city budget. The board of education has its own budget. When it can't raise enough money, it decides where to cut costs. Maybe you know that some cities lately have dropped school sports, killed the school paper and drama clubs, and so on, because there wasn't money for them."

"Gee, I hope that never happens here," I said. "Where does the school board get money?"

"Mostly from property taxes—that is, taxes on land and houses and other real estate."

That night at dinner I asked dad if our city's taxes are high.

"They sure are," he said. "But maybe they have to be. I

can't think of any city services we could do without."

"What kind of taxes do you pay? Just sales taxes and property taxes?"

"Let's put it this way. Practically every time I spend money, a tax is added. Other taxes are taken out of my paycheck before I ever see it. Then I have to send in a check for my state income tax, plus another check to Uncle Sam's tax collector. Hey, why this sudden tax talk?"

I explained the merit badge I was working on.

He nodded. "Every citizen pays taxes and should know what he pays for. But let me warn you, Mike—don't get an idea that people are always right to be kicking about taxes. They may be right or wrong. A tax is simply a citizen's share of the cost of government. If he doesn't get his money's worth, he'd better help improve the government."

"How? Citizens don't decide how much they'll be taxed, do they? And they don't decide where to spend the tax money."

"In some places tax plans are on the ballot for citizens to vote on. In most places the tax program is up to the government. But at least the voters elect the people who do decide the tax program. Every place gets the kind of government it deserves. Somebody else said that, but I sure agree. You see, I haven't time to study how much we ought to spend on the police, the fire department, sanitary inspections, and all the rest. That's why I help elect a city council to do the studying. When they hold public hearings to get other viewpoints, maybe I'm too busy to go and join in the discussion—or I think I am. If they decide wrong while I sit home and leave the decisions to other people, I've got no kick coming."

"What do the councilmen do after you elect them?" I asked. "How do they decide how much tax they need?"

"**They ask** every department how much it needs. How much to keep up the city parks? How much for streetlights and sewer repairs? How much for the dog pound,

for the garbage trucks, the civic auditorium? When they add up all these costs, they know how much they need to collect in taxes. The next question is how to spread the taxload as fairly as they can."

"Why not share and share alike? They know how many people live in the city. Just divide the money they need by the number of people."

Dad grinned. "Think it's that easy? How would you pay your share?"

"Well, you'd have to pay my share. I meant every family should pay the same. That's fair, isn't it?"

He asked me, "How about families who are out of work? How about a widow supporting 10 children? Lots of poor families hardly have enough money to buy food."

I scratched my head. "Probably the city needs a list of families who are rich enough to pay their share."

"Plus the share of the others," he added. "And it's not easy to find out how much money each family has. They don't all brag how rich they are."

"Maybe the tax collectors can tell by the way people live," I said. "How they dress. The cars they drive. Clues like that."

"That's just what they did in the old days," he said. "They judged how rich a man was by the number of windows in his house. When bathrooms came in, that was a measure for taxing. But nowadays they send expert appraisers to figure how much each house is worth. They decide what price it would sell for. Then the houseowner is taxed so many dollars for each hundred dollars his property is worth."

"But what about people who don't own property? Lots of them can afford to pay taxes."

He chuckled. "True enough. You aren't the first to notice it. Remember, no one is exempt from paying their share of taxes. People who rent are taxpayers, too. Apartment owners add taxes to the rent.

Additional tax money comes from the city charging various fees. It charges for a marriage license or a dog license or a building permit. It may collect a coin or two from everyone who crosses a bridge or uses a toll road or parks on a busy street. When someone breaks a city law he usually has to pay a fine. It all helps to cover the city's costs."

"What if the costs get real big—in an emergency, maybe?" I asked. "If the city ran out of money, would it close down the police department or stop fighting fires?"

"It might come to that in the end," he said. "Some public schools really do close for lack of money. But first the city would try to borrow the money. That's what a bond issue is. The voters must okay it. If they vote no, there can't be a bond issue. A bond is a promise to pay later, plus good interest—and the payments come out of taxes in the end."

"Is that why my school didn't get enlarged? A bond issue didn't pass?"

"Right. The school board agreed we needed a bigger school, but it didn't have enough money. So it suggested issuing school bonds. In the last election, the citizens voted against this."

"Which was a darn shame," I said. "Still, if people don't want something enough to pay taxes for it, I guess they've got a right."

"Sure. But maybe property taxes and bond issues aren't the best way to pay for schools. A city with mostly poor people is likely to get poor schools that way, although poor kids need a good school as much as anyone. By the time you're a voter, you may be voting on new tax ideas."

"I guess I'll be taxed plenty, one way or another."

"No doubt. If a citizen wants services from his community—and that's why he lives there—he can't escape taxes. But it's up to him to elect people who'll make sure his tax money is well spent."

Doing Your Part

7. Show that you have taken an active part in elections of your officers and matters of business in groups to which you belong.

I wasn't too happy when my Uncle Jack stopped in for dinner with us one night. He's red-hot for Scouting, which could mean trouble for me. I knew he'd ask questions during dinner.

It was troop meeting night, but I didn't plan to go. Sure enough, Uncle Jack asked me, "How's your troop going?"

"All right, I guess." I kept my eyes down.

After awhile Uncle Jack said, "You don't seem exactly crazy about your troop, but do you mind if I go with you and watch the meeting?"

I had to break the news sometime, so it might as well be now. "I'm not going. I've decided to quit."

Mom gasped. "Mike! What's wrong?"

"Nothing. I'm just tired of it."

"But Son," she said. "You have had so many fine experiences. And you've saved up to go to summer camp. You can't just quit like this."

"I'm sure he has reasons. Give us the lowdown, Mike," Dad said.

"Oh, mostly it's this little king, this senior patrol leader, Paul Mayes," I said. "Anybody can see the Otters are Paul's favorite patrol. He gives them 10 points in honor patrol contest for every little thing they do, like coming in with a new yell. But no matter what my patrol does, Paul hardly ever gives us a point."

Dad nodded thoughtfully. "That isn't all, is it? What else is wrong?"

"Well, we haven't had a hike or a camp in months. Why should I stick around when there's no excitement?"

I wished everybody would just let me alone, but Mom wouldn't.

"If your senior patrol leader isn't fair, surely something can be done. Maybe your father can speak to the Scoutmaster. Don't you think Mike should stay in the troop, Jack?" She appealed to my uncle.

Uncle Jack shook his head. "It's Mike's own business. I'm disappointed, but maybe Mike just doesn't have what it takes."

I glared. "That's not true. I'm working on a tough merit badge. I haven't missed a patrol meeting. There's nothing wrong with me, it's the troop."

"Yes, you were a pretty good Scout, I thought," Uncle Jack said. "You seemed to be getting a lot from the Citizenship merit badge, but evidently it didn't sink in. You didn't get the idea at all. You don't know what citizenship means."

"You just ask Judge Wise! He'll tell you I know a lot!"

Uncle Jack growled, "You may know lots of answers. But you're flunking the real test of a citizen. The test is what you do."

"Well, I do all I can," I said.

"Nuts," he said. "What would your father do if he thought the city council wasn't fair? Would he just quit—leave town?"

"I guess not," I muttered.

"What would he or any good citizen do?"

"Well, maybe he'd go to the city council and argue," I said. "He'd try to get some changes made."

"Sure," my uncle snapped. "And that's the difference between you and him. Your dad is a good citizen. You aren't. You just quit."

He turned away and smiled briefly at my mother. "Thanks for dinner. I'll be going. Good night."

I decided to go to the troop meeting after all. When we got into patrol corners, I asked the patrol leader, "Can't we do something about this point contest, Mark? Why not ask Phil for a list of ways a patrol can get points? I think the troop should vote on a list."

The whole patrol felt the same way—including Mark, who promised to bring it up at the troop leaders' council meeting.

"And can you find out when the next camp will be?" I suggested.

He nodded again. "I was wondering myself."

He got results. I was surprised how easy it was. A week later we found a list of contest points on the bulletin board, ready for voting. A schedule of monthly camping trips was posted too. I guess all our troop needed was some good active citizens like me.

Volunteers for Service

8. List and describe the work of five volunteer organizations through which people of your community work together for the general good. Do something for or take part in the activities of one of these organizations other than Scouting.

I showed Judge Wise my list of five organizations: the Rotary, Kiwanis, Optimist, Lions, and Exchange clubs.

"You certainly took the easy way," he said. He didn't sound pleased.

"Is there something wrong with my list?" I asked. "Aren't those good examples of organizations that work to help people?"

"Your examples are all good. But they're too much alike. They all are called service clubs. Most of their members work in downtown offices. These clubs all have weekly lunch meetings. They all spend some time on projects to improve the community."

"I can tell you projects they've done," I said. "Rotary bought a bus for the Boys' Club. The Lions built a dining hall for Scout camp. Another club takes crippled children to ball games—"

"It was easy, wasn't it?" he broke in. "You probably got all you needed in a 10-minute talk with your dad."

"Well, yes. Didn't I do enough?"

"You've done enough to pass the requirement, just barely. But you would have learned more about being a citizen if you had scouted around to find five or six *different* kinds of citizens' organizations, instead of just taking five that are the same kind."

"Why does everybody think I'm looking for the easiest way?" I said. "I'm not afraid of work! If you could please give me some clues to different kinds of organizations, maybe I could make a list you'd like."

He smiled. "Fair enough. Let's see what clues I can think of. This city is just swarming with different kinds of organizations that give their own time and money helping other people." He jotted on a pad, then handed the pad to me. He had written:

"What are some organizations that work on disease, that help people in trouble, that help educate children, that study local government, and mainly help the community by raising money for charities?"

If Judge Wise thought he would stump me, he was wrong. I've been around town, on my paper route and on jobs downtown where I deliver circulars. And I've read newspapers, since I started this merit badge. So I could answer most questions on the pad as soon as I looked at them.

"Disease problems? There's the Heart Fund, the American Cancer Society, and so on," I said. "Helping people in trouble? The Salvation Army—and how about Travelers' Aid, at the bus station?"

"Good examples," he said. "Keep going."

"Organizations to help children? The PTA, of course. And some churches and synogogues have their own schools. The YMCA runs some classes—and how about the Scouts? Couldn't you say Scouting helps educate us?"

"Sure it helps," he said. "Well, Mike, you're aware of more civic groups than I thought you were. Try the other questions on my pad."

I looked again. "Organizations that study local government and try to help it run better? I've heard of a Citizens' Budget Commission in town. And there's a Taxpayers' League that asks questions at city council meetings. And isn't there a committee for urban renewal? Maybe it would work with the city government to improve housing and living conditions."

Judge Wise said, "I was thinking especially of the League of Women Voters. It studies local governments all over the Nation. And it tries to find facts about local questions that people vote on. Then, too, in our city and many others, an organization called Town Hall meets once a week to listen to a talk by some outstanding expert on a public problem."

I looked at the next question and tried to think of a teen-age organization. Finally, I told the judge I didn't know any, except for high school clubs which I figured were mainly educational.

"I'll give you a hint," he said. "The city hospital desperately needs help everyday, because doctors and nurses can't do all the little side jobs."

That rang a bell. "I know! When Dad was in the

hospital I visited him. I saw boys and girls helping there, doing errands, and I guess they talked to anybody they thought looked sad. Are they an organization?"

"Yes, an organization of high-school kids," he said. "They're an Explorer post that specializes in hospital work. . . . Didn't you notice lots of ladies helping?"

"You mean besides the nurses? Oh yes, I saw some dressed differently. Who were they?"

"Probably an organization called the Red Cross Gray Ladies that helps at many hospitals. Or it might have been the women's section of one of the veterans organizations like the American Legion—or maybe a women's group from one of the churches."

"Lots of groups help hospitals, don't they?"

"Yes, but much more help is needed there," he told me. "You might look into it sometime."

But why not do something more—something for the hospital, if it wanted me? I talked to Steve, and he suggested our whole patrol might take on some project for the hospital.

Judge Wise was saying, "We haven't mentioned a lot of quite different volunteer organizations like the Family Service associations; or the Friends of the Public Library; or the Needlework Guild that makes clothes for poor families; or the Youth Employment Service that finds summer jobs for boys and girls; or the adoption agencies that place orphans with families who want children. We haven't mentioned the YMHA or CYO, or the organizations that specialize in helping blind people or drug addicts or people in other trouble."

"I don't know about those," I said. "But I know that all the kids in town are better off because citizens do a lot for us in their spare time."

"And it doesn't cost a cent of the city's money," Judge Wise said. "Did you ever stop to think how much higher our taxes would be if the government had to pay for everything that is done to help people?"

"Well, at least I know that Scouting doesn't run on tax money, and neither does the Boys' Club or the YMCA or the Campfire Girls," I said. "Where does their money come from?"

"Out of the pockets of volunteers—citizens who decide to help," the judge said. "Volunteers not only give service, but they give their own money, and ask for money from other people who can't give time. In fact, there are some volunteer organizations that concentrate on raising money which they divide up among many different charities. This brings us back to the last question I wrote on my pad."

"I've never heard of organizations like that," I said.

"Oh, I think you have. Didn't you ever hear of the community chest? the United Way of America?"

"Oh, I heard of them, but I never knew what they were. I should know, because my mother goes out every year to ask people to give to the UWA."

"**All right then.** There also are other organizations that work hard raising money which they give away. Fraternal lodges like the Moose and Eagles do a lot of this. So does an organization called the Junior League. You may not have heard of it because its members are all ladies, but its money helped to build half the camps and basketball courts here."

I said, "I guess all the really good citizens spend a lot of time working for free, helping the community in different volunteer organizations. Is our Scout executive a volunteer?"

"No, Scouting is his full-time job, and he gets paid for it," the judge said. "He may give spare time to working in the Rotary club and in his church and other organizations. He's a volunteer for them. But for Scouting he's a professional—he's like a professional athletic coach or movie director, except that his job is to train Scout people instead of athletes or actors."

"I never see him training our Scoutmaster," I said.

Judge Wise laughed. "Scouts never see one-tenth of what a Scout executive does nor one-tenth of the men who are active in Scouting as volunteers. Any volunteer organization as big as Scouting needs a few full-time professionals, who work mostly behind the scenes. That's why a church hires a minister; why your school board hires a superintendent of schools. In fact, it is also why a city council may hire a city manager, if the city councilmen are only serving part time."

"Well, anyway," I said, "am I okay on Requirement 8? I didn't take the easy way, did I?"

"I'd say you took the hardest way, with a little steering from me," he chuckled. "We'll make a good citizen out of you yet, Mike."

Politics and Public Service

9. Do one of the following:

  (a) Name the main political parties in your community or state. Explain their different points of view on one public issue.

  (b) Describe one job in your community in some form of public service. Tell what qualifications you need for the job.

"Are you a Republican or a Democrat?" I asked Dad when I started this requirement.

"When it's time to vote, I pay less attention to political parties than to the men they've nominated."

"What's the difference between Republicans and Democrats?" I asked.

He thought a minute. "In some parts of the country, many people think that the Republican Party mostly favors business, and that the Democrats mostly favor the workingman. But that isn't always true by a long shot. Some Democrats do a lot to help business. Some Republicans want to put tighter controls on business. And both parties have helped bring more prosperity to lower paid people."

"I'm mixed up," I said. "Do you mean that both parties are pretty much the same?"

"No, there can be big differences between them in any one city or state or on an important national question that clearly divides them."

"**I still don't** get it. How can I tell a Republican from a Democrat?"

"Only by what he calls himself. You can't tell by his ideas about government. He may be a right-winger, a left-winger, or in the center and still be in either party."

"Right wing? Left wing? Sounds like hockey."

"Well, in the grand old game of politics, if you're in the right wing, that means you aren't in favor of many new ideas. Right-wingers are conservatives; they usually stick to the older ways of doing things. But if you're on the left, you're pushing for new ideas, for big changes. Some people would call you a radical."

"And if I'm in the center, what does that mean?"

38

"It means you listen to both sides, and sometimes vote for changes, but not very big changes. You might be called a liberal or a middle-of-the-roader."

"**Why aren't all** the right-wing types in one party and the left-wingers in the other?"

"Well, Son, you might study for years and not find a clear answer to that question. American politics just grew into other patterns. I think we're better off because our political parties are so flexible. With conservatives and liberals in each, both parties give a hearing to all viewpoints and new ideas. And both parties can shift to meet changes in public opinion."

I thought of Bill Bryan, a Scout in my troop. His father works in the city attorney's office.

I said, "Dad, you know Bill Bryan? He says his father is a Democrat because the Bryan family has always been Democrats. He's great on loyalty to the party. Is that bad?"

Dad shrugged. "Mr. Bryan is in politics, and party loyalty is important among politicians. I certainly wouldn't criticize him for it. He might not get far in his party if he didn't work hard to help elect the party's candidates. But to me, a political party is a bunch of people who get together to raise money for election campaigns. They do this because they want to elect certain people. As a voter, I'm mainly interested in what kind of man they put up for office. I want to know his ideas, and the party label doesn't tell me."

I showed Dad the merit badge requirement. "How can I explain the parties' points of view on one public issue if the parties are so blurred and changeable?" I asked.

"You'd better pick a local issue or a state issue," he said. "It could be a tax plan or some question about the schools or colleges or some proposed new law. When the election campaign starts, watch the newspapers and TV, and you'll soon get an idea of differences between Democrats and Republicans on that one specific point. Every candidate will probably take a stand on it."

"Next election is a long way off," I said. "I'd better do 9b instead. I can talk to Mr. Bryan about his job, or to Judge Wise about being a judge. They'll tell me how I could prepare for those jobs."

"Okay," Dad laughed, "if those are the jobs you want. But don't forget the one you know the most about."

I stared. "I don't really know anything about any job in public service."

"How about Scouting?" he said. "The Scout executive does a public service job. He helps in organizing troops, Cub Scout packs, and Explorer posts, running camps, advising leaders, raising money, planning camporees and Scout-o-ramas. I understand his pay compares well with other jobs in public service. Why not ask him about the qualifications you would need for his job? You might like it even better than being a judge."

Your Community's Water Supply

10. Do one of the following:

   (a) Draw the course of your home water supply from watershed to water tap and on to receiving stream. Show waste treatment, if any.

   (b) Find out if the water supply is likely to be a problem in your town in the future. Explain why.

11. Define water pollution. Give the main causes and results of water pollution nationally and in your town. Find out what steps, if any, are taken to control pollution in your area. Tell what other steps might be taken.

I could write a big book, if I were a writer, about water problems: how to get enough water, and how to keep it clean enough to use. I found this was a hot subject all over the country as soon as I mentioned Requirements 10 and 11 to Judge Wise.

"Water supply is likely to be a problem in almost any community within the next few years," he told me. "I happen to know that more than a thousand American cities have had to cut down on water at one time or another within the last few years—turning off water for certain hours daily, for example, or passing laws against watering lawns. I'm not sure how we're fixed for water in this particular city."

"How can I find out?" I asked.

"The city waterworks or the city engineer's office in city hall can help you map where our water comes from and where it goes after we flush it down the drain. The map will help the experts show you whether we may run short and why."

"You mean this town might turn into a desert or a ghost town from lack of water?" I asked.

"There's enough water in the world for everyone,"

the judge said. "Engineers can bring in enough—for a price. If there's a shortage here, it just means our water bills may go sky-high."

Judge Wise gave me another tip. He said that the Audubon Society is campaigning all over the coun-

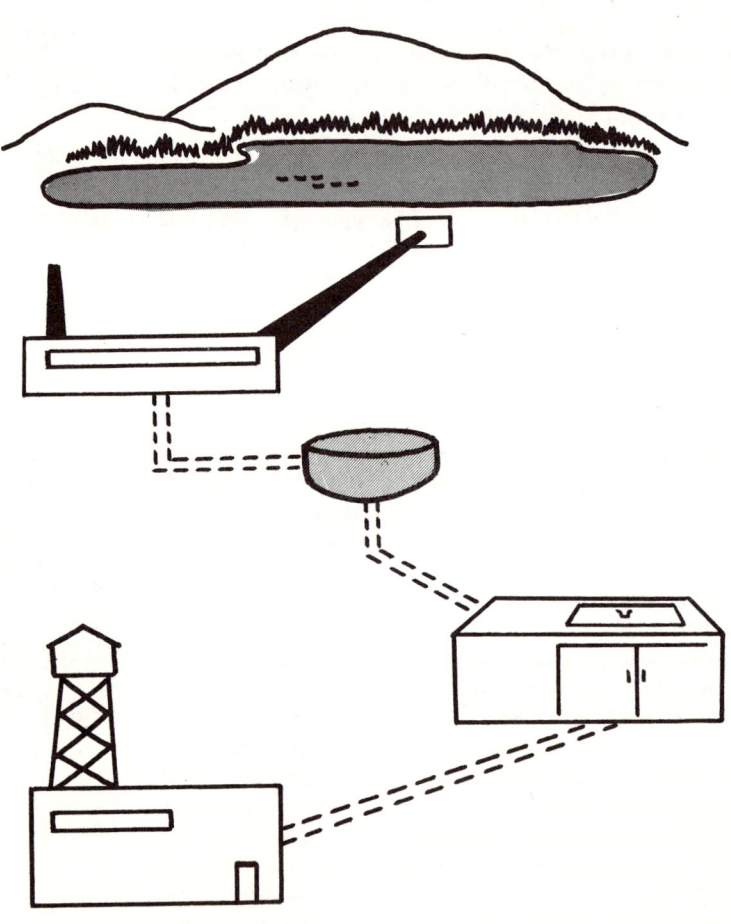

try to stop water pollution. At the public library I got the address of an Audubon Society chapter nearby, and it told me plenty about pollution.

In fact, it shook me up. I read a statement from the chairman of a U.S. Senate committee warning: "Well before the end of the century most Americans will be drinking, cooking with, bathing in, and otherwise using secondhand or thirdhand water." I thought this might be all right if the water got purified each time we used it. But then I found that the sewage from one-fourth of all the people in America is poured into our water supply without any treatment at all. No wonder I've seen news about outbreaks of typhoid and hepatitis blamed on contaminated drinking water. All 22 of the U.S. river basins are polluted, if what I've read is right.

I asked one of the Audubon people if much was being done.

"Oh yes," he said, "the country began getting serious about clean water in 1965. Congress passed laws putting the power and the money of the Federal Government behind states and cities to help them build sewage plants. That's what we'll need: thousands of big chemical works, like factories, to clean the water before it goes back into a river or lake."

"So now our worries are almost over, right?" I asked.

"No, the job is just starting. We won't see much difference in our big bodies of water for at least 10 years," he said.

"Why so slow?" I asked.

"It takes years to get such plants built—to get the city council to vote, get the land, fight the lawsuits, sell the bonds. Many, many cities haven't done much yet. The last time I checked, only about half of America's municipal sewage systems were giving any treatment to sewage before pouring it into a stream or lake. And there are many industrial plants that still make water unfit for fish or men by pumping their wastes into it."

"They'll have to spend a lot of money to clean up our water," I said.

"Just purifying the water they themselves use will cost them millions—which means they'll have to raise the prices of whatever they sell. Some factories won't buy expensive water-treatment plants until they're pushed—and some cities won't either. We citizens will have to keep pushing."

Planning for Land Use

12. Tell how good land-use planning is important to five of the following: community planners, highway builders, camp planners, small landowners, farmers, ranchers, recreation planners, industrial and housing developers, fishermen, and hunters.

This was the hardest requirement for me to understand. I was no community planner, highway builder, or any of the others. I live in a city and expect to stay. Why should I know about land use?

I asked Steve. He knows a little about it, since he's ahead of me in school and reads more.

He said, "The trouble is that almost everybody needs to live in a big city or its suburbs. I read somewhere that our cities add, as many people each year as if we'd dumped Philadelphia into them. In fact, two-thirds of all Americans are now jammed into 16 huge-city areas which keep growing like cancers. The farm towns are dying out. It's hard to find jobs anywhere except in big cities or nearby."

"Then we may wind up with a few supercities and nothing else, by the time I get out of school," I said. "Maybe I'll move away and be a hermit."

"Maybe a lot of people will move in the next 10 years," Steve said. "Plenty of big companies are already moving their offices and factories way out of town into the countryside."

If all these moves into and out of the cities change the maps, my future may look different than I thought. Maybe uses of land are going to be important to everybody.

To find out, Steve and I went to an office of a regional planning commission. When we explained what we needed, a man sat us down by his desk and started talking:

"By the time you boys are my age, you might be living in a United States as thickly populated as Europe. What will we do with all these people? Where will they live, work, play?"

"I hope they don't keep swarming into the cities," Steve said. "The cities are too crowded already."

"Right now the big growth is in the suburbs around the cities," the man said. "Each year, bulldozers chew up a half-million acres of open land around the suburbs to meet needs for new homes, new factories, more highways, bigger airports, more reservoirs, and the like."

"**Couldn't people** spread out more evenly into the wide-open spaces?"

"That's exactly what we want to happen," the man said. "In the next 10 years, we hope, there'll be as many as 350 small new cities, no bigger than Seattle or Louisville, scattered across the 97 percent of America that is empty. The Federal and State Governments are trying to help this happen."

"I guess you need a lot of advance agreements, then," Steve said.

"Sure. Where will each new road run? Where will the new schools and hospitals be? How can we persuade industries to move?"

"Some industries make a lot of noise and smoke," I said. "Does every town have to have factories and mills?"

"No, many towns could have a college or a scientific center. Others could be vacation resorts—maybe a boat marina or a ski run or a dude ranch."

"Sounds good," I said. "There's nothing to prevent all this from happening, is there?"

"It's happening now in some places. But people can interfere in other places. For example, a vacation area can be spoiled if someone builds the wrong kind of factory nearby or starts a real estate subdivision. A dam in the wrong place can change a plan completely. Or a new town might get so cluttered with cars, filling stations, motels, bars, shops, and apartments that people wouldn't want to live there."

"I heard of other things going wrong, too," Steve said. "Cropland can go bad because of strip mining or overgrazing or bad farming."

"Yes. About one-third of all American topsoil has been blown away or washed away so badly that nobody can reclaim it," the planning man said. "Plows and cattle did most of the damage."

"But there's still plenty of land for farms and camps and industry and housing developments and everything else, isn't there?" I asked.

"Yes, there is, if people will just agree on what should

go where," he said. "If they don't, then farmers may ruin a water supply by spreading insect-killer on land that drains into the water. Or a highway may ruin a wooded area for campers or fishermen or hunters. On the other hand, if the highways bypass a new city, it could die like the small towns bypassed by the railroads a century ago."

"Does the owner of land always have the final say about how to use his land?" I asked.

"**No, most often** it's up to the voters in the end," he said. "Sometimes it takes new laws or a new governmental body to control the use of land. Sometimes it just takes a county board of supervisors or a state legislature to pass a zoning regulation. Sometimes everything depends on whether a town grants certain building permits, or says 'Keep Out' instead."

"In other words, the citizens have to get a plan made and followed," Steve said.

"That's it. So if you want to be a good citizen and make America a pleasant country to live in, you'd better work for plans that will use land for the benefit of many people."

Your Community and You

13. Do the following:
    (a) List and explain at least five privileges and forms of protection you enjoy as a citizen in your community. Describe your obligations to the community.
    (b) Plan your own program of community service. Get approval of your plan from your Scoutmaster and counselor. Give 5 hours of your time in carrying it out. Or, give 5 hours of community service carried out by your Scouting group.

By the time I got to this, weeks had passed since my first visit with Judge Wise. We argued about whether an 11-year-old was really a citizen. Most of what he said was still in my head, so I could name my "privileges and protections as a citizen."

The judge wasn't satisfied. He made me tell about the different kinds of workers paid by the government just for the benefit of citizens.

"Now what about your obligations?" he asked.

"I already know about paying taxes," I said, "and going to school. Is there anything else?"

"A community is a huge team of many people and organizations helping each other," he said. "One of your obligations is to help keep the team running, so everyone gets help and protection. How can you do that?"

"Obey the laws?"

"**Yes, that's** one way. If too many citizens broke laws, the teamwork stalls. Anything else you can do?"

"I guess I ought to play on the team myself. With all these volunteer organizations and citizens' groups, there must be ways I can help."

"Sure there are," he said. "And it's up to every citizen to find ways of helping. Have you found any?"

I told him about my troop's service projects. "I've already put in more than 5 hours," I said. "That's what Scouting is all about."

"And it's what citizenship is all about—playing on the team, carrying your share of the load, keeping alert for chances to improve something.... All right, Mike, you've earned a merit badge. Come back when you're ready for Citizenship in the Nation."

Books About Citizenship in the Community

Recommended by the American Library Association's Advisory Committee to Scouting, 1972

Scout Literature

Citizenship in the Nation, Citizenship in the World, Communications, Public Health, Scholarship merit badge pamphlets.

Other Books

Bixby, William. *A World You Can Live In: Our Ecological Past, Present, and Future.* David McKay, 1971. $4.25.
   Ecological problems in our technological society are reviewed, and channels of action are discussed.

Hellman, Hal. *The City in the World of the Future.* M. Evans, 1969. $4.95.
   Urban accommodation as viewed by the architect, engineer, and urban planner confronting new demands on rapidly changing environments.

Hoag, Edwin. *American Cities; Their Historical and Social Development.* Lippincott, 1969. $4.95.
   Historical treatment of the growth of cities, with a brief discussion of contemporary problems. Excellent bibliography.

McCoy, J. J. *Shadows Over the Land.* Seabury Press, 1970. $4.95.
   Aspects of pollution and other ecological problems are discussed in terms of civic prevention and cure.

Markun, Patricia Maloney. *Politics, a First Book.* Franklin Watts, 1970. $3.75.
   All levels of government affect and are affected by the local community through the many channels of the political process.

Stevens, Leonard A. *How a Law Is Made: The Story of a Bill Against Air Pollution.* Crowell, 1970. $3.95.
   From its origins among individuals, concern for a pollution problem is traced through the legal process.

Stevens, Leonard A. *The Town That Launders Its Water.* Coward-McCann, 1971. $4.49.
   A California community copes with water pollution.

Worth, Jean. *Man, Earth, and Change: The Principles and History of Conservation.* Coward-McCann, 1968. $3.64.
   The history of conservation and its importance to 20th century man, including legislative means of action.